Education and Creativity

Simon Foxell and
William J Mitchell

**black dog
publishing**
london uk

By the year 2025 the climate will have changed irrevocably, mainly as a result of greenhouse gas emissions. The temperature is predicted to be, on average, half a degree warmer and will fluctuate to a greater extent. Rainfall will have reduced but will also become more extreme. Resources such as energy, water and food imports will be in shorter swupply and transport will be constrained; partly as a result of climate change but also due to regulations aimed at preventing global warming. In this series of important and timely books the Edge explore the impact these changes will have on our lives in the future. Global in scope and far reaching in its implications this series examines the significant social, environmental, political, economic and professional challenges that we face in the years ahead.

Contents

Education and Creativity in the Light of Climate Change
Robin Nicholson

Introductory Edge Scenario

The knowledge and creative economies will be the key to the continued success of UK plc. But with significant changes in the demographic mix and higher social expectations the ability and opportunity to both learn and employ new skills will need to extend to embrace all sectors and ages of society. The ability to problem-solve and cope with a fast changing world may become highly prized; the ability to teach this even more so.

Notes for a Briefing

The difficulty of looking back from 2025 to 2008 is
highlighted by recalling where we were in 1991–1992 and
our inability to foresee the events that then took place.
In 1992 we were into the second year of John Major's
premiership and the second major Tory recession; the
power of the trade unions, including the teachers' unions,
had already been emasculated by Margaret Thatcher
and her adopted monetarist ideology. Much public
sector expertise had been lost through the progressive
reduction of funding and Compulsory Competitive
Tendering of Local Authority services. The public
estate was continuing to run down through the lack of
maintenance over the tenure of many governments. The
minimal detailing and maintenance and the extensive
single glazing of 60s schools made for rotting elevations
and high levels of discomfort in both summer and winter:
but talk of designing for climate change was still strictly
for enthusiasts.

In the following notes I briefly consider the ever-changing
purpose of education; the range of pedagogical styles
and the variation in school sizes; the progressive take-
over of education by Big Capital; the growth of the
knowledge economy and our collective failure to foster
new cross-disciplinary learning and practice; the change
of scale from relatively local to being both more global
and more local as a result of ICT; the desire to transform
the school into the social hub of the community; and the
change of life-style, including the resulting epidemic of
obesity, in response to social and climate change; and
finally the challenge of the creative economy.

Looking back?

Historically the religious orders and their institutions
provided education in pursuit of their own interests
with many of the great monasteries they established

continuing to flourish as Universities and Colleges. From the sixteenth century on there has been a growth in the number of significantly different faiths practised in the UK with increased sectarianism particularly flourishing in times of war and pestilence. Confronted by the continuing threat of climate change we are likely to see further polarisation and threats to our liberal traditions.

While education has been useful for maintaining social control and for developing basic skills for the factory and other work, there has always been a countervailing interest in developing individual creativity, with visionary pioneers such as Dr Maria Montessori who started working with so-called 'abnormal' children in 1899 and went on to found a world-wide movement. The aim of the Montessori Movement is to "place all the children in our world at the centre of society and to assist them in becoming the transforming elements leading to a harmonious and peaceful humanity". Other pioneers included; AS Neill, who carried out his long experiment with many so-called 'difficult' children at Summerhill; and Henry Morris who set up Impington Village College in the 1930s.

Impington Village College, designed by Walter Gropius and Maxwell Fry, is still a thriving establishment, with 1,347 pupils aged between 11 and 18, in a village just north of Cambridge. Henry Morris was the Secretary for Education in Cambridgeshire from 1922 and his concept of the Community School remains just as powerful 100 years later. He brought together the School, the Village Hall, the Reading Room, Evening Classes, Agricultural Education Courses, the Women's Institute, the British Legion, the Girl Guides, the Recreation Ground, the branch of the County Rural Library, the Athletic and Recreation Grounds; all in a way we still strive towards today.

In 1997 New Labour was elected partly on the strength of a commitment to "Education, Education, Education". Their education policy included the aim of getting 50 per cent of the UK population into Higher Education. One casualty of this was the continuing devaluation of craft skills, although many leading professionals remain grateful for the creative potential that was unlocked by the process and discipline of designing and making.

Starting in 2005 the New Labour government launched the ambitious Building Schools for the Future programme with the commitment to rebuild every secondary school in England. The aim was to have started the reconstruction of at least three schools in every education authority in England by 2016. In 2007 the government started moving towards making them zero-carbon. Success in carbon reduction has been more successful than many expected once it was accepted that the generation of renewables on-site was bad value and the major opportunity of cooperating with local communities began to develop.[1]

1 In an article in *Building* magazine 24 August 2007 Bill Watts, senior member of Max Fordham and member of the Edge argued that the cost of providing 60 per cent of requirements from renewables for a 10,000 m² secondary school on site would be in the order of £3.5 million whereas 100 per cent from a remote wind-farm could be provided for between £250,000–£500,000.

However the multi-activity model instigated by Henry Morris has proved more elusive as a result of the continuing silo-mentality of so many authorities.

There have always been many styles of teaching, many subdivisions by age or ability and many sizes of school ranging from; the individual programme at home, Small Schools of up to 100 to the education campus with say 2,400 pupils.[2]

2 www.smallschools.org.uk

3 www.thecademy.net/inclusiontrust.org/Welcome.html

Whatever the format, there remain a substantial number of children who absent themselves from school for economic reasons or because of bullying. In May 2007 the Observer reported that 100,000 pupils were missing from school; although this was balanced with a report on the successes of the 'Not-School' programme which provides a personalised 24 hour learning service for 1,000 children through mentors in the UK and New Zealand.[3]

Growing anxiety has also been expressed in 2008 concerning a rise in truancy from the increasing number of larger schools.

The knowledge and creativity economies

The growth of the information revolution, the impact of Information Technology and the rapid growth of the Creative Economy became a major area of interest for the DCMS and other government departments following pioneering work by Richard Florida and Charles Leadbeater and think-tanks such as ippr and the Work Foundation. Education had previously been delivered at a relatively local level but ITC allowed access to knowledge to be on both a more open global scale as well as maintaining its local strengths.

The shift in access to information at a global scale can be compared with the move towards world-wide acceptance of the policy of Contraction and Convergence where there was an acceptance that, in order to prevent climatic catastrophe, a reducing amount of available carbon needed to be shared equally between all people. This response to the threat of climate change and the opportunity of Knowledge Sharing engaged the whole world cooperatively for the first time, although not without plenty of argument, struggle and profiteering along the way. At a more local level a greater sense of community through sharing local power generation, waste disposal and use of water began to be experienced in many parts of England.

Inter-disciplinary education

Although the UK recognised its dependence on the knowledge and creative economies long ago, we must wonder why we continued to organise our learning institutions, especially our universities, around nineteenth century subject baronies, policed by professional institutions. This approach has been particularly acute in the planning, design and construction professions amongst many others. By restructuring the form of the urban university one or two institutions began to encourage both cross-disciplinary knowledge creation and engagement with local and business communities. One side-effect of this greater physical openness has been to help make the community a safer and more enjoyable place in which to live and work: be it in the city, small town or village. However it took a long time for the social and creative aspects of Further Education Colleges to be recognised and life-long learning to be valued as it is, once again, today.

Inter-disciplinary education and practice in the construction industry has long been recognised as a key with government reports championing cooperation and partnership at regular intervals. In 1988, under the leadership of the engineer Ted Happold, the Construction Industry Council was set up to bring the whole construction industry—clients, designers and constructors—closer together. Previously in 1976 he had been appointed Professor of Architecture and Engineering Design at the University of Bath; he established there the pioneering joint teaching of architects, structural engineers and, crucially, environmental engineers. Having produced a generation of professionals who could think in a cross-disciplinary way, this approach faded away only for the challenge to be taken up in other places and other sectors.[4]

4 In 2008 the Warwick Digital Laboratory opened with a multi-disciplinary team covering ten disciplines which have been offered to other departments in the University, the local business community and the NHS to develop all matters digital.

Given the free-thinking traditions of the UK it is difficult to understand the extraordinary resistance to crossing academic boundaries and to allowing pupils of all ages to teach themselves, singly and collectively. One example of this resistance saw, in 1989, the abandonment of a validated proposal for the future of the Prince of Wales

Institute of Architecture to redefine itself as a mid-career urban design and regeneration hub. This was proposed as a high-achieving mid-career masters' course where the 'students', drawn from finance, planning, design, construction, private and social housing and local government would teach one another on a part-time basis. The Institute would have merely facilitated and administered the course—but it was not to be.

Sustainability and Health
It has proved helpful to consider CO_2 as waste, that is something that does not add value, just like empty drink bottles (in the early part of the century two million plastic bottles were being thrown away every five minutes in the US) and construction and demolition waste in the same period every year in UK up to 19 million tons of new construction materials were brought to site but not used and were taken to landfill).

Many parents found themselves being criticised by their own children for the waste they created. The 'eco-school' programme achieved remarkable success in raising awareness of climate change and understanding the concept of responsible citizenship.[5]

5 www.eco-schools.org.uk/

By 2010 it was becoming more widely accepted that the school could become a key agent for changing our understanding of carbon, water, waste and bio-diversity and for changing of our behaviour to be more cooperative. With a wide-spread panic about the rising cost of obesity (ten per cent of the NHS annual budget by 2010) the school also became a focus for exercise.

So where do we go from here?
Many have forecasted the importance of transformational change in education at all levels. It is now backed by a growing appreciation of the need for cross-disciplinary creativity and facilitated by affordable ICT.

The rapid growth of change in our climate has affected us all differently depending on our latitude, our geology and our topography. The world-wide nature of this change has required a world-wide approach to avoid the conventional outcome of scarcity resulting in war. Much has already been achieved but new targets for reducing our impact on the planet and for increasing our productive activities continue to be urgently necessary.

If one is an optimist one can see the threat of climate change continuing to be an opportunity however the dark forces of Big Capital, competitive religions and the unfair distribution between the haves and the have-nots continue to make us question such optimism.

Education and Creativity
Simon Foxell

It has been 20 years since the introduction in December 2007 of The Children's Plan by the then Labour government.

Although the original offered more-or-less a business as usual approach it has since become a useful benchmark to measure the subsequent change in education policy. While this report provides an overview of that change it does not attempt to go into detail or take sides in any of the many academic debates that have raged in the period on this topic.

The report looks at three levels of policy drivers that have forced or encouraged change.

1   The immediate and pressing: characterised as 'Panics'. These were usually triggered by one-off events or a perceived series of events, picked up and pressed home by the media and anxious politicians.

2   The medium term and foreseeable: characterised as 'Policy and Planning'. Ideas and challenges emerging from think-tanks and expert groups. Often political in content and planned out in advance—if not always perfectly.

3   The longer term and unavoidable: characterised as 'Overarching Change'. Driven by global political, social and environmental change, but not always seen coming or planned for.

Inevitably there is a degree of overlap between these three levels and it is anticipated that the reader will tolerate some repetition as well as the necessary gross simplification.

2007–2008

Ten years into a government that had been elected on a mantra of "education, education, education", results were shaky and change had been slow to arrive. Despite major programmes aimed at under-achievement, literacy, numeracy and behaviour and ultimately the wholesale renewal of the secondary school estate through the Building Schools for the Future programme, there was a perception that things were not getting any better. The media had plenty to get exercised about, from struggling learners, burgeoning numbers of school refusers and the obesity of the child population, but even an ever-increasing exam pass-rate wasn't seen as a success, but instead as the evidence of "falling standards"and grade inflation. Money spent on education by the government was portrayed as "wasted billions".[6]

6 For example: Gove, Michael MP, *Parliamentary Debate*, 17 December 2007: For example: Glover, Stephen, *Daily Mail*, 13th August 2007

UK governments had not held back on initiatives to improve educational performance and had passed an Education (or similar) Act every year since 1992 (only excepting 1995), perhaps justifying the complaints of perpetual revolution and death by reorganisation. Education had become one of the big beasts of the political menagerie, apparently always hungry for more policy initiatives and electoral promises from politicians only too eager to feed it and relieve its evident legislative malnutrition. Adequate funds to accompany the new requirements were always in short supply. Only the Building Schools for the Future programme promised, or threatened, to break this pattern.

Building Schools for the Future was (and remains) the UK government's plan to rebuild or renovate every secondary school in England over a 15 year period from 2005–2006 at a then estimated cost of £45 billion.

The programme was accompanied by the firm intention to transform educational delivery:

> At the heart of Building Schools for the Future (BSF) is the need for local authorities (LAs) to develop a vision for education in their area that offers real innovation and enables teaching and learning to be transformed. It is the first principle of a successful BSF strategy.[7]

7 DfES, 2004

What the idea of transformation meant at the time was far from clear; but now, as the programme approaches its likely end, it begins to be possible to make an assessment not only of what was achieved following the opening of the first BSF school, the Bristol Brunel Academy, 20 years ago in September 2007, but also what was understood by the notion of educational transformation, before the onset of the international and technological challenges of the last two decades began to hit home.

The 2004 Children Act together with the publication of the suite of "Every Child Matters" (ECM) papers changed the focus of much of education in England; even though many similar pastoral approaches were already in place across the country. The view that the education system should be designed around the needs of learners rather than schools and teachers was, remarkably, radical for its time and the implications of that shift in focus is till being worked through as facilities are renewed and reinvented. The ECM approach was central to the idea of educational transformation, but it took some time before it was seen to be as equally applicable to the requirements of mainstream pupils as it was to those with special needs and the gifted and talented.

> Children and young people have told us that five outcomes are key to well-being in childhood and later life—being healthy; staying safe; enjoying and achieving; making a positive contribution; and achieving economic well-being. Our ambition is to improve those outcomes for all children and to narrow the gap in outcomes between those who do well and those who do not.[8]

8 *Every Child Matters: Change for Children*, DfES/HM Government, 2004

The core principle that developed this thinking into real change, was "personalised learning" Born in September 2003 when Tony Blair used the phrase in his annual speech to Labour's Party Conference in Bournemouth describing a vision of "personalised learning for every child in new specialist schools and city academies".[9]

9 Speech by the Prime Minister, Tony Blair, to the Labour Party Conference, 30 September 2003

Personalised learning has gone on to have a life of its own, possibly very different from Blair's original intent. Much interpretation and spin followed the Prime Minister's speech, including a certain amount of rubbishing by sceptics: "The whole thing is a duplicitous gimmick. In reality, schools just do not have the resources, time or the space in the curriculum to implement it."[10]

10 Gilbert, Francis, *The Times*, 11 April 2004

But even in 2007–2008 it meant pretty much what anyone wanted it to mean, although commitment to the broad principle was becoming firm:

11 *The Children's Plan—Building Brighter Futures*, DCSF, December 2007

> Personalised learning puts children and their needs first. The Children's Plan sets out how we move to a more sophisticated approach to personalisation making it standard practice across the system.[11]

The transformation agenda and the impact and development of personalised learning will be discussed under "Policy and Planning" later in this book.

Also coming to the fore in 2005–2010 were the early stirrings of action to deal with the impact of climate change. The UK government had signed up to hard-hitting targets: reducing carbon emissions from 1990 levels by 20 per cent by 2010 and 60 per cent by 2020, but more critically the environment was beginning to exert its own pressures. These included the heat wave of 2003 and the summer floods of 2007.[12] Schools were seen as a key player in the government's policies and not only because the many thousands of school buildings were understood to be significant users of energy:

The education sector accounts for approximately ten per cent of carbon emissions for all commercial and public buildings.[13]

But also because of the educational potential inherent in making schools demonstrably carbon neutral:

Renewable energy technologies have a key role to play in reducing carbon emissions and engaging future generations with climate change issues. The use of renewable technologies can also provide a rich learning resource for teaching of science, geography, design and technology, citizenship and mathematics.[14]

The means to achieve these targets were less than clear at the time, especially in the education sector where flexibility over the use of buildings was very constrained by externally imposed factors including; the custom and practice of school days and three term years, public exam timetables and contracts for after-hours use of school premises and facilities. It was not surprising that these constraints were to be effectively dismantled within a few years of the effects of climate change biting.

12 The Environment Agency has identified nearly 5,000 infrastructure sites in England and Wales where the flood risk is greater than one in 75 years. This includes 2,215 power stations and sub-stations, 737 sewage and water treatment works, 680 health centres and surgeries and 401 schools." *Summer Floods 2007: Learning the lessons.* Association of British Insurers November 2007.

13 *Climate Change the UK Programme,* DEFRA, 2006

14 *Climate Change the UK Programme,* DEFRA, 2006w

Internationally, the UN's Intergovernmental Panel on Climate Change (IPCC) had stated that "warming of the climate system is unequivocal", but the UN climate conference in Bali later in the year, despite leading to a global consensus on the seriousness of the threat, achieved no agreement on action.[15]

15 Summary for Policymakers of the Synthesis Report of the IPCC Fourth Assessment Report, 16 November 2007

The impact of climate change on education and schools policy will be discussed further in "Overarching Change".

Although much international attention was distracted by the occupation of Iraq, the continued growth of China was noted, albeit mainly in terms of its consolidated role as much of the world's, and certainly the UK's, manufacturing centre. In a similar vein, India was recognised for its import of call centres and information processing from the UK. What was still to be felt was the challenge to the UK from both these huge economies to the knowledge economy jobs that were rapidly becoming Britain's best hope for continued growth.

The knowledge economy is also emerging as a key driver of the restructuring of international trade in some advanced economies towards high value added services. Over the past decade we have seen a boom in UK exports of services associated with the knowledge economy such as financial services, computer services, business services, and royalties and licence fees.[16]

16 Brinkley, Ian, *Defining the Knowledge Economy*, Knowledge Economy Programme Report, London: The Work Foundation, 2006

The same 2006 report from The Work Foundation noted the relative lack of investment in the UK (3.7 per cent in 2002) into this sector—a lack of investment that would critically affect the success of UK education in preparing for a creative, knowledge and service based economy in the years ahead.

The OECD has produced a composite indicator of "investment in knowledge" made up of investment in R&D, investment in higher education, and investment in IT software.

By this input measure, we can identify three groups of economies:

- High knowledge investment economies of North America, OECD Asia and Japan, investing around six per cent of GDP.
- Middle knowledge investment economies of Northern Europe and Australia, investing between three and four per cent of GDP.
- Low investment economies of Southern Europe, investing between two and three per cent. of GDP.[17]

The shift to knowledge-based economies and the subsequent backswing will be discussed further in "Overarching Change".

17 Brinkley, Ian, *Defining the Knowledge Economy*, Knowledge Economy Programme Report, London: The Work Foundation, 2006, p. 7

Panics

Politics, driven by the ever-shorter news cycle and in recent years by the direct and powerful mobilisation of virtual mobs; ready to exert pressure, almost instantly and without warning on any subject; has been more prone than ever to succumb to decisions made in the heat of media cauldron; a phenomenon now known as "doglaw" (after a panic in 1990–1991 over pit bull terriers mauling babies). Owing to the inevitable presence of children in Education; this sector, of both society and politics; has been more affected than most by the power of panic.

The following are a few examples from the past two decades:

2009–2010

The OECD's authoritative PISA (Programme for International Student Assessment) survey of the knowledge and skills of 15 year olds and including data from 65 countries, indicated that the UK's overall reading performance had fallen back by 17 points or almost the equivalent of six months in school age. The Koreans and Poles, who had improved their score by 31 and 29 points respectively between 2003 and 2006, had added a further 12 and 13 points in the following period bringing them to the top of the reading table. In Mathematics the UK had now slipped behind Turkey to 39th place. The Finns continued to lead in science, but the UK was now only just managing an average in the OECD scores. A no-confidence vote was held in Parliament on the competence of the government.

The government survived by a slim majority but the entire ministerial education team was replaced, followed by internal restructuring of the Education Department. The government promised (without eventually delivering) a new educational policy modelled on Korean practice and with an emphasis on learning by rote and mastering the facts. Schools responded instead by concentrating resources on their best and most promising students and keeping lower performers from progressing to test thresholds. Results improved; allowing the government to be re-elected and brought local authorities and schools some freedom to pursue their own policies. The incident temporarily damaged the move towards personalised learning, but by challenging its tenets and providing the opportunity for teachers to take stock, it may have strengthened it in the longer term.

2012–2013
The failure of Great Britain to secure a single gold medal for athletics in the London 2012 Olympic games was roundly blamed on schools and their failure to inculcate a spirit of individual drive and competition in young people. The issue was twinned with the growing obesity problem in the collective consciousness, by the death of an overweight participant on a TV reality show in the early Autumn.

In response the Secretary of State for Education introduced a daily 'exercise hour' into the curriculum and he was filmed taking part in a ten mile cross-country run with his family. It later transpired that he had only joined the race for the last mile and the subsequent media furore resulted in ministerial resignation and a cabinet reshuffle. The exercise hour played havoc with curriculum planning, with under-resourced schools struggling to find the staff or facilities to fulfil their obligations. The popularity of active sports declined further.

2015–2016

A child abduction from outside the gates of a school in the suburbs of Manchester triggered a series of copycat attempts as well as a number of accusations against "strangers" observed "too close" to schools. The press reported daily on sightings of the missing child and all and any other developments. One accusation got out of hand as a passer-by was 'stoned' by an angry crowd and was seriously wounded. Parents besieged school gates and insisted on increased security around schools. Private security companies moved into the sector. Ministers were forced to react and embraced and championed a Private Member's Bill requiring all children up to age of 16 to be fitted with a GPS tracking device.

Other aspects of the positional devices rapidly became standard features within schools and they became used as registration and attendance monitors and to ensure proximity-based security for the use and loan of ICT equipment. Exercise and diet were tracked by the system, with remedial action taken as required. When students were missing from lessons at which they were due, attendance officers were alerted and were sent out to collect them. Ministers acclaimed an overwhelming success tackling the formerly intransigent problem of those not in education, employment or training (neets). The system was enthusiastically sold to countries across the world.

2017–2018

Oil prices had been rising incrementally, little by little, for well over a decade and had roughly trebled to over $300 dollars a barrel in ten years. The cost of other energy sources; gas, electricity and biofuels of various sorts; had all kept pace. The impact had been considerable as businesses and people had gradually changed their behaviour to minimise expensive travel and unnecessary heating or cooling, and had begun to invest in dedicated renewable supplies. But despite all the pulling back on usage and increases in efficiency, the system had reached a point when the cost of energy had become greater than any monetary benefit gained from its use. And yet the economy had to keep moving. It was a crisis waiting to happen and needed only a small incident to trigger it. That incident occurred in February of 2018, when a refinery outside Rotterdam had a minor fire and closed down its capacity for repair. Panic struck and rapidly spread to struggling producers as well as consumers. The spot price for oil soared; producers held back their limited supplies waiting for even better times; Russia used the opportunity to apply political leverage and restricted gas supplies to the international market; and the global energy supply infrastructure stalled and then froze, tipping the world into a potential crisis.

The implications for education were not immediately clear, but the limited moves that the UK had been making towards energy security suddenly became urgently prioritised in every sector. But, and specifically as a result of the zero-carbon requirement of the later Building Schools for the Future waves, the few working examples of energy self-sufficient sites in the UK were approximately one thousand school premises scattered across the country. The sector became the shining example of the way forward. All other schools were ordered to match such best practice, the curriculum was rapidly re-written to focus on energy issues and schools were immediately required to offer programmes to educate and re-skill everyone, children and adults alike, in 'energy-zero living'.

The shockwaves from 2018 were considerable and even now the world is still coming to terms with the implications, even through the world's systems were restored and fully running again within the relatively short period of approximately three months.

2018–2019

A summer heatwave in June, with temperatures rising daily above 30°C for over a fortnight, and with peak temperatures on several days over 35°C, made conditions in the majority of schools in England intolerable. Schools were closed for the remainder of the summer term. The public exam schedule was upset for the third year in ten years and public complaints reached a crescendo.

Following a similar, but milder, chain of events in 2016, the Education Select Committee had produced a report on the reordering of the school year, the findings of which the government gratefully accepted and passed in law by the end of the year. Not since the Great Stink of 1858 had a government acted so fast in response to the effects of a hot summer. The result was a radical dismantling of the three-term school year. In its place was instituted a flexible year of 1,000 hours that could be taken at times to suit both learners and schools, together with a modular system of assessments. The new system had been the result of years of planning and partial trialling by a dedicated group of academics, teachers, local authorities and politicians, but it had taken an unexpected and unplanned crisis to achieve its adoption.

2024–2025

A combination of global market forces, unaffordable transportation costs and a series of April hailstorms resulted in a severe food shortage across the country throughout the late summer and autumn. There were riots in supermarkets and distribution depots and food security became the central issue in the emergency General Election called by the government in November 2024. The political parties vied with each other for policies that would achieve the promise of the Prime Minister that "Britons would never have to go hungry again".

The policies that won the election for the opposition party were the calls for a 'return to the land' and an 'end to waste'.

Local government was required to ensure local food and resource availability and short and robust supply chains. The national curriculum was rewritten to include time spent learning to grow crops and the principles of farming and market gardening. Practical skills of maintaining and repairing equipment were also included as was an entire new and compulsory module in life-skills for a zero-energy economy.

The new school timetable came into its own at this moment of perceived national crisis. Learning modules could be taken at moments that fitted with the more urgent need to provide for the family, to spend time guarding the allotment and queuing at the food market. Practical skills could more usefully be learned in workshop settings and many employers offered their services as skills mentors. The 'spirit of war-time' was invoked regularly by people and politicians alike, although few could remember the war they were referring to.

Policy and Planning
Educational Transformation and Personalised Learning
In part, the greatest educational success of the past 20-plus years has been the transition from a system based on institutions; and institutions doing what institutions do best; to one founded on the idea that learning is done by individuals; individuals of all ages and levels of attainment. It has been a gradual process, a process neither smooth nor complete, yet ultimately one that has profound implications for all those services that support learning.

In its early days the focus was on improving the lot of those who had been let down most badly by the system; those with greatest need and the most vulnerable in society. The Every Child Matters agenda had originally emerged from the scandal following the torture and death of the eight-year old Victoria Climbié in 2000 and was focused on ensuring that the multiple agencies that had contact with her should act in future in an integrated and joined together manner.

Every Child Matters: Change for Children in Schools states:
"Integrating services should mean more effective support for
pupils with complex needs who require multi-agency support."[18]

Support for the longstanding concept of personalised learning
followed logically from the ECM agenda as the needs of older
children were considered, but in its initial form it was largely
focused on closing attainment gaps. As the 2005 Education
White Paper, Higher Standards, Better Schools For All, noted:

> To drive up standards while also improving social mobility,
> we are determined to provide more personalised services
> for children and their families. Personalisation is the key to
> tackling the persistent achievement gaps between different
> social and ethnic groups. It means a tailored education for
> every child and young person, that gives them strength in
> the basics, stretches their aspirations, and builds their life
> chances. It will create opportunity for every child, regardless
> of their background.[19]

But just as an early desire to provide access for the disabled
eventually became the principle that high quality and equal
access should be provided for all, whatever their levels of
ability: so with education. We now understand the principle
of personalised learning as providing the best and most
appropriate learning environment, resources and guidance
for everyone. And with that understanding came a welcome
reinvention of what schools could be and were for.

The idea of personalisation was being actively explored in 2003–
2004 as a proposition for creating value in the public sector by
the new and upcoming generation of Cabinet Ministers. This
found a particular voice in a Demos report, *Personalisation
through participation* published in 2004 with a Foreword by
David Miliband, the then Minister of State for School Standards:
"The recipe of 'basics plus personalisation' may not trip off the
tongue, but it speaks to real need and real aspiration."[20]

18 *Every Child
Matters: Change for
Children in Schools*,
DfES, 2004

19 *Higher
Standards, Better
Schools For All*,
DfES

20 Miliband,
David, Foreword,
*Personalisation
through
participation*,
London: Demos,
2004

And it was to the education sector that the idea spoke and found its home:

> Personalised learning would provide children with a greater repertoire of possible scripts for how their education could unfold. At the core there would still be a common script—the basic curriculum—but that script could branch out in many different ways, to have many different styles and endings.[21]

21 Leadbeater, Charles, *Personalisation through participation, A new script for public services*, London: Demos, 2004

With political support and funding, for the principle, the detail began to be worked out by those schools and Local Authorities most enthusiastic about moving education into the new century and equipping learners with the best education for facing the challenges ahead. It was soon obvious that the idea meant not only a new approach to teaching and to school buildings and facilities, but to the curriculum, assessment, discipline and behaviour as well:

> Headteachers, teachers, pupils and parents who have been involved in thinking through what they want their school to be like in the future have found that the task is a far more complex one than simply designing a new building. They have needed to define the learning and teaching, the relationships and the behaviours that they want to see. Using the whole school site and designing spaces that will promote new ways of working is only part of the process.[22]

22 2020 Vision Report of the Teaching and Learning in 2020 Review Group, 2006

In a personalised environment, serried ranks of rooms suited for marshalling groups of 30 no longer made sense. Similarly, the idea that a year cohort progressed at the same rate across all subjects; always a difficult proposition—whatever the weather; simply and finally broke down, as did annual testing and public examinations at predetermined ages. As soon as the principle of personalised learning took hold; then reinvention of learning; of teacher training; of school facilities and environments; naturally flowed from it and resulted in the turnaround we have seen in the past two decades.

The idea and pursuit of change was slow and difficult at first.
The teaching profession had, after all, come through a period
of constant reinvention and had only recently returned to many
of the principles of 'best practice' with which they felt relatively
comfortable. The latest change was sold with protestations that
it represented standard and even better practice:

> Personalised learning is not a new initiative. Many schools
> and teachers have tailored curriculum and teaching
> methods to meet the needs of children and young people
> with great success for many years.[23]

23 www.standards.
dfes.gov.uk/
personalisedlearning/
about/

> Some of the best schools and the best teachers are already
> demonstrating what these aspirations mean in practice.
> However, for them to be achieved for all children and young
> people, in all schools, all of the time, there will need to be
> changes both to the way the education system operates
> and to the practice of many teachers.[24]

24 2020 Vision
Report of the
Teaching and
Learning in 2020
Review Group, 2006

But in reality it was a difficult sell, simply because it represented such
a significant change; not only to the way schools addressed learners
and their needs, but also the relationship between teacher and
learner to the physical space in which learning was achieved. Spatial
requirements were confused with ideas of adaptability and flexibility
of space; almost as if sliding or folding back walls could, by the
power of metaphor alone, open the minds of learners and trigger the
ability to self-direct their own education. There were lessons to learn
from the world of office design, where the walls had been dispensed
with in the 1970s and 80s to be replaced with open plan layouts, but
they probably weren't that space should be in permanent flux.

More powerful was the appreciation that to provide personalised
learning a school needed to provide an environment where
each individual would be recognised and greeted as a person,
and their day-to-day requirements for identity and belonging
provided for. In return they might be expected to contribute to
their immediate part of the school community, to act responsibly

and with a sense of discipline. The members of such communities might, and perhaps should, be a diverse group; of different backgrounds, cultures, sexes, abilities and ages, able to help each other as well as themselves. It was important, if not critical, to get the social setting right to allow learning to flourish, perhaps even before considering what was to be learnt.

Such communities by themselves were too small to provide for much of the shared expertise and facilities needed in schools; specialist teachers and dedicated know-how, science and technology spaces, gyms and sports hall, theatre and performance spaces, etc., although the creative use of ICT was changing even that. But several learning communities might come together to make up a larger group, able to share resources and when necessary act together as one, larger unit.

The only significant research into performance and school size in England (Spielhofer, et al, 2002) found that: 'performance improved with size up to a certain school size, then declined. The best results were obtained in medium sized schools (with a cohort of approximately 180–200 pupils), and the worst in the very small or very large schools.' However, they cautioned that 'the observed impact of school size, although statistically significant, is quite small'.[25]

25 Kimber, Mike, *Does Size Matter? Distributed leadership in small secondary schools*, National College for School Leadership, 2003

The move to new ways of learning was both supported and driven by the capacity of new technology. Computers and devices of many varieties allowed access to expertise, the ability to work, produce and invent, to communicate and to record experience in almost any setting. The freedom that books had offered to the relative few who would happily spend a day lost in a library searching for nuggets of information, was suddenly available to the many; and almost instantly. Images and sounds became as accessible as words and phrases; to capture, recall and control; enabling those with strong non-linguistic intelligences to engage and create work in all subject areas and outside the traditional confines of the art and music rooms; and be as expressive as those whose skill was primarily with language.

The anywhere, anytime capacity of ICT drove, above anything else, the change in learning. It came with its own inescapable logic that change was inevitable and had to be embraced and taken advantage of. ICT was, as it remains, only a facilitator of knowledge, but one with an ability to pull even the most reluctant along in its wake. The early days had been full of 'youth-orientated' attempts to make it interesting and relevant to learners, but they turned out to be both irrelevant and unnecessary. The positive feedback of discovery and achievement was enough on its own to engage almost anyone. Learning was just as possible, with guidance, from a small screen in a quiet corner, as it was from the teacher at the front of a classroom; from making a model out of wet paper and clay or from a group performance; but the best education was achieved, from a mixture of many different styles adopted and adapted at the most appropriate time for learning.

It was the potential of ICT that fully enabled the project of transformed education/personalised learning to spread across the majority of UK schools and for some of them to ultimately decide to become open schools. The idea of anywhere, anytime was adapted by schools and made available to those learners able to take on gradually increasing responsibility for their own programme of work. The aim was for schools to provide a secure place, a home from home, where a wide range of learning experiences and resources was available; critically including individual learning guides and mentors as well as friends, peers, collaborators and competitors. Degrees of freedom were individually calibrated and negotiated for each student along with daily and weekly achievement targets as well as longer-term goals.

Other developments, including the introduction of Global Positioning System (GPS) tracking linked to the national identity register, despite its distinctly Orwellian character, allowed more pupils to spend time outside school, learning in the workplace, at home, at other schools or elsewhere. It also permitted schools gingerly to open their facilities to other learners as their presence and identity would be checked and monitored. Equipment became more mobile as it too was tracked and would only work in proximity to personal tracking devices. It became possible for a school to monitor the location of any piece of equipment and who was using it.

The freer education system that emerged from the transformation process was not for everyone. Many still needed a rigid environment in which to operate and learn, and in well-organised schools this was easily provided with a gradated scale of freedom, responsibility and licence for those learners able to make it work for them. Personalised learning needs to provide different solutions for the wide variety of learners in different subjects and at different stages of their learning path.

Such a range of provision initially caused chaos with curriculum organisation, as far wider ranges of options opened up. This has since settled down with the discovery that freedom of organisation cuts both ways and reasonable solutions to timetable planning could be developed much as before. Increased use was made of play-again facilities via interactive learning platforms, as well as the ability to access other teaching materials, lectures or on-line lessons covering the same topic. The same materials could also be revisited for revision and updating.

By 2020, transformation to personalised learning had taken root in almost all schools that had been through the later waves of the Building Schools for the Future programme, along with many others from the earlier waves. It had developed different forms and was expressed and explained in many ways. But there was always, at the core of each version, the consistent idea that the pupils' needs came first and that the purpose of schools and the education service was to help them develop their potential and abilities to the best of their capacity and to the benefit of their later lives as well as to society as a whole. And although it is too early to have gathered authoritative evidence, there is also a growing belief that the latest generations of pupils are more self-confidant and assured, and potentially more entrepreneurial; better able to make their own way in an increasingly threatening world.

The shocks of the international events of 2017–2019 on domestic issues confirmed the status of the approach in many minds. Personalised learning had shown itself to be a robust system with the resilience and flexibility to survive multiple simultaneous demands on its ability to function. It had been a 'big idea' in the early years of the century, but it had since gathered its own momentum out of the media and political spotlight, and had transformed the traditional school service into one that could rapidly adapt to the latest demands on it.

A number of schools across the country have taken the process further by developing an open school movement, reducing their provision to that which they were best able to provide and sourcing as much of the learning experience elsewhere as possible. They share their resources and expertise between themselves and others as far as they can. In conscious emulation of the open source movement they encourage input and improvement from whomever is willing to contribute. The movement is very aware of the fine balance there is between risk and reward in the freedom and openness they advocate and practice and are vigilant in protecting not only their students' safety and security but also their need for freedom to explore society's boundaries.

International Pressure
It is only in the last few decades that international comparisons have meant a great deal in education. Models of education have been exported from one country to another for centuries but despite their influence they have not competed, as they do

now, to produce the best students for higher education or for the most lucrative jobs. Previously a country could develop the most appropriate, or inappropriate, education system for its own purposes and not have to worry that students from other systems might win away economic capacity or supply graduates world-wide. International education league tables now play a major role in regional economic success and capital flows.

As global companies look world-wide for competitive advantage they are, as ever, searching for cheap manufacturing bases with easy access to *entrepôts* on the trade routes for the new clipper network, but they are also looking for intellectual and creative resources to develop their products and brands and to sell services and on-line expertise. China and India have excelled in recent years in this. They have broken out of traditional mindsets, just as the Japanese did in the 1970s, to become global players not just in manufacture but also in the creative and service- and knowledge-based sectors.

Many argue that this became an economic necessity after global trade collapsed following the oil crisis of 2018. But both countries and many nations in Eastern Europe and the ASEAN block had been preparing to move on from their successful, but relatively low profit, manufacturing base since the turn of the century. Higher education had been refocused to ensure a supply of high quality graduates capable of competing world-wide.

The oil/energy supply crisis in 2018 forms a distinctive break point in the 20 years of our survey. Up until that year, global trade, not only in goods but also services and soft skills, had been in rapid expansion, following the trends established in the 1980s and then re-energised by the collapse of the Soviet Union and its satellites from 1989 on and the opening up of China and the far East in the following years.

By the Millennium the new model of global capitalism was being treated as if it was a permanent condition. Jobs in manufacturing and information processing were exported to economies with cheaper labour rates, leaving the UK economy with a sole remaining strength—in the service sector. The impact on education policy was to produce more and better highly skilled graduates in order to protect the increasingly vulnerable nature of this position. As noted by the Higher Education Policy Institute in 2003:

> It is encouraging that the policy focus on skills is becoming wider. Only by taking this broader view will we be able to "reach a proper understanding of the inter-relationship between skills, knowledge and organisational performance and to devise policies that could help move the UK towards becoming a high-wage, high-skills, high-productivity economy" (Keep and Mayhew, 1998). The stubbornly low demand for high-level skills and their utilisation in the UK needs to be given equal focus to the supply of high-level skills.[26]

26 Aston and Bekhradnia, *Demand for Graduates: A review of the economic evidence*, Higher Education Policy Institute, 2003

What was envisaged was an educational arms race based on keeping the UK ahead of its competitors in high-level skills, innovation and creativity. Economic competitiveness had been purged sector by sector from the UK economy over a period of three decades, as it became more cost efficient to manufacture and then carry out clerical and information processing tasks elsewhere. The UK's only option was to ensure that the service economy kept its edge and global market share and remained as profitable as it was in 2007 when the OECD reported on the UK economy:

> Globalisation, together with skill-biased technical change, is changing the composition of jobs in advanced economies and raising the level of skills required to do them. This has increased the importance of educating a large proportion of the population to much higher

standards than in the past. The government has responded to this challenge by raising education spending and expanding the capacity of the education system in key areas such as pre-primary education and increased participation in education beyond the age of 16.[27]

27 *Economic Survey of the United Kingdom*, OECD, 2007

The collapse in global trade following the 2018 energy crisis meant that this policy was never truly tested. The first cohort of children to enter a BSF school aged 11 in 2007 had barely emerged from further education when, briefly, the only goods available became those already stockpiled or those produced and manufactured locally, and a new chapter opened for the UK economy. Together with the food crisis of 2024–2025, events forced a change of emphasis to more immediately practical matters, especially of energy conservation and generation, food supply and regional manufacture. Change was seen as necessary in educational policy to match the new priorities but to date political energies have been focused elsewhere and in any event restructuring finance is unlikely to be found.

Unlike many Western economies the UK revealed a high degree of resilience and has stood up to the global knocks reasonably well. The policies instituted to achieve the targets set in Kyoto in 1997 and Copenhagen in 2009 stood the country in reasonable stead. Schools in particular, especially those built since 2010 when the zero-carbon requirement became effective, are still functioning well as semi-autonomous and reasonably self-reliant entities despite the temporary failure of their external ICT platform. The global trade in services continues to be healthy, based on the high-speed data links installed at the start of the century, although economists are still puzzling over how to transfer monetary value in a world of relatively little global trade in physical commodities. Even trade looks set to be on the increase again now that the clipper service is expanding its network and capacity.

Recent events have set in train a new direction for education in the UK. One based on practical skills and above all creativity. In part this has been expressed in the strong interest in agriculture and mechanics but most remarkably in systems engineering and the desire to learn about the operation of complex natural systems. Behind all these individual subject shifts there lies a determination to gain the ability to acquire new skills as the external world throws out new challenges. There appears to be a real appetite to learn from the brushes we have had with global economic collapse.

With global communications working reliably again after the partial breakdowns at the end of the last decade, the world has effectively achieved an inversion of nineteenth century trade patterns. Then commodity exchange dominated the world and global politics; even the closed Kingdom of Japan was forced to open with the arrival of United States Navy ships in Uraga Harbour in 1854; but communications across the world were tenuous at best. Today instant communication is straightforward but the transportation cost of high volume, low value goods has become prohibitive. A recognisable value system has been turned on its head and the world of education has had to scrabble to adapt to the new priorities.

Despite this upheaval the relatively new personalised learning system has proved remarkable robust. As a system it was intended from the outset to deal with a constant level of change and to be able to adapt almost weekly to new circumstances. It was, after all, the one thing that all the commentators agreed on at the millennium—that the new century would be one of constant and accelerating change. The personalised approach was always intent on teaching the ability to learn and to problem solve, and although in its early stages creativity as a necessary tool for life in a changing world was noticeable by its absence from policy documents, that was remedied fairly rapidly by schools themselves in response to the concerted demand from universities for students who could think productively and imaginatively for themselves.

The following article written by Professor Bill Mitchell, director of the Design Laboratory at MIT describes his thinking back in 2007 on teaching creativity. It is interesting to consider how much of this approach has found its way into contemporary learning methods and how much we still have to learn.

Overarching Change. Climate Change, Peak Oil

Some of the immediate effects of climate change and global warming have already been discussed but given the growing significance of this issue to British and global society and therefore to education since the start of the century it is impossible not to give it its own section.

The warnings had been clear enough: from authoritative bodies like the UN's International Panel on Climate Change, to the economist Nicholas Stern and the former US Vice President Al Gore, as well as many lesser-known names. All pleaded with the world, its countries and individuals to take action before climate change became irreversible and dangerous.

But although it dominates our lives now, the subject of climate change only reached the UK's National Curriculum in February 2007:

> The education secretary, Alan Johnson, said: "It is inconceivable that young people growing up today should not be taught about issues like climate change —it has enormous relevance to their lives. Children not only learn about our future, they shape it.[28]

28 *The Guardian*, 2 February 2007

Since that time climate change's position in the curriculum has kept on rising and covers not only the issue itself and explorations of its impact across the world, but training in the many measures that are necessary to adapt to its effects and avoid its worst dangers. The series of crises that it has provoked; from malaria outbreaks to food shortages and weather that can veer from drought to flood within a few short months; are all used as learning tools as well as being challenges to the management of schools. Like the rest of the economy schools do well to continue in the face of these regular 'emergencies'.

Two major effects of climate change, in particular, have had a significant effect on schools: the first has been the increase in immigration, largely from countries whose infrastructure has collapsed under the strain of failing crops and changes in disease patterns. The UK's multi-cultural society, generally operating successfully in the early years of the century, has struggled to accommodate the recent influx. But the education system, from several decades of experience, was relatively well equipped to provide for the many non-English speaking children and families who arrived; predominantly from Africa but also from many other areas of the tropics. In return immigrant communities brought many skills for dealing with life in extreme climates. No-one would pretend though that this hasn't been a huge challenge for schools, not least in areas of previously settled immigrant communities, some now in their fourth or fifth generation.

The other major change, as noted above, was the nearly universal move away from the 9.00–3.30 school day and three-term year. The logic for a change, one that had long been championed for educational reasons, only became compelling when environmental conditions forced a move to morning and evening school and to more equable times of the year. The timetable change also opened the opportunity to follow the module-based curriculum that is now the norm across all schools.

Schools across the country now operate at times to suit themselves and their local community and are negotiated to suit the changing patterns of everyone's lives, growing seasons and the increasingly common habit of the midday siesta. Most schools are now open year round from early morning to late evening for different groups of learners and to provide a wide range of local services. A few have started to offer 24 hour availability.

Knowledge

Even 20 years ago the world had become a place where certain forms of knowledge were instantly available to both general and specialist seekers. Search engines and expert systems provided such efficient information retrieval and management, that knowing facts was becoming little more than an impressive skill to be shown off in pub quizzes. However, *The Economist* magazine could still tease potential readers with marketing slogans such as; "You can't know everything about everything… but you can give it a good go."[29]

29 Advertisement for *The Economist*, 2007

The potency of the advertisement was provided by the assurance that such a quest was, in truth, futile, and that there were better ways to approach knowledge than needing to know it. This was already becoming true 20 years ago when it became unnecessary to memorise phone numbers or to retain mental maps once an in-car satellite navigation was installed. But since then, with the invention of the e-Mem device in 2020 and its mass-marketing in the years following, maybe it has just become possible again. Use of the device has overthrown the idea of knowledge as an educational end in itself and changed people's approach to knowledge entirely.

The personal memory device (the e-Mem) was developed as a simple storage extension to normal brain activity. The availability and expanding capacity of digital memory capacity (a doubling every two years if Moore's Law 26 is to be believed) was ideally suited to provide for the demand this generated. The brain needed to be trained to use the new device, but once working it proved remarkably adept at reliably holding and providing instant retrieval of anything consciously memorised to it. A market has since evolved in ready-made knowledge supplements that can be simply downloaded to increase an e-Mem's stock of information. Other products are in development.

With the device in place, knowledge became rapidly differentiated by users between the codifiable, which could be stored, and other tacit forms; manual and mental skills, intuition, judgement, emotion etc.; that could not. There was surprise, outrage and condemnation when it became clear where the dividing line between these forms was discovered to lie; but the proposal to ban the device stood no chance against its obvious popularity and manifest usefulness.

The effect on the education system was to strengthen further the change agenda—to push harder at developing the so-called soft skills and, in particular, the ability to think and to create. In many ways the development of the e-Mem has crystallised the purpose of learning for a least another generation. René Descartes would have been more than pleased at the outcome.

Conclusion
Education has come on a roller coaster journey in the last 20 years, but the changes instituted in the early years of the century have been shown to be remarkably robust in surviving all that has been thrown at them.

The Building Schools for the Future programme established in 2004 has now, almost, run its course. It was intended to have been completed by 2020, but has done reasonably well in being due for completion in 2030. Surprisingly, the political will has stayed with the project despite changes in governments and the severe battering by events. It has been enormously costly and the Unitary Charges local authorities are paying to the consortia, or more typically their more financially acquisitive successors, who built or rebuilt all those schools through the life of the programme are now dominating local authority budgets almost to the exclusion of anything else.

The schools completed 15–20 years ago are now showing their age and desperately require substantial upgrading, but any chance of more money being found at this time of harsh cost cutting seems remote. Why the UK never moved to a programme of continuous school building and improvements, always preferring feast or famine, is a question as baffling now as it was 20 years ago.

The transformation of 'education' into an effective system of 'personalised learning'; a process which took immense effort from a wide range of educationalists to make it common practice; once modified by practice and adaptation, has shown its value. That, in the main, was because it was designed to be flexible and adaptable; a policy for a century almost predicated on change, but a surprising triumph nonetheless. The immediate beneficiaries, the children and students who experienced an education system tailored to their individual needs, include the generation that are now starting, in turn, to transform society, business and the arts. Their achievement will speak for itself.

Creative Networks
William J Mitchell

These days, global digital networks are crucial enablers of education and creativity. And they are fundamentally transforming long-familiar strategies of teaching and learning.

The nineteenth century model of professional education, for example, went something like this: first, you spend some years in an atelier or professional degree programme to acquire a stock of intellectual capital; next, you are examined on your mastery of that accumulated knowledge, and if you pass you are then licensed to practise; and finally, you do practise your profession for several decades—drawing on your intellectual capital, and occasionally topping it up by reading or attending professional development seminars. The trouble with this, in a rapidly changing world, is the underlying assumption that you can know what you need to know in order to be a competent problem-solver in some domain.

But this assumption is increasingly tenuous. It seems to me, for example, that most of the really interesting and important design problems and innovation tasks that I encounter these days don't fall neatly within established professional boundaries, but instead sprawl messily across them. In the recent design of a new urban mobility system by my research group, for instance, we had to deal with the structural, mechanical, and electrical systems of vehicles, the configuration of urban infrastructure, and the structuring of new kinds of markets for electric power, road space, and parking space. We had to consider what functionality to embody in hardware, and what to accomplish with software. We had to explore tradeoffs between carrying systems in moving vehicles, and offloading them to the fixed infrastructure. Who is trained and licensed to handle all that? And this condition is not unusual; it is increasingly typical.

The usual response is to create a large, multi-disciplinary team of specialist consultants. But the rigid division of labor and responsibility that this entails—although sensible and useful for detailed design development—is the enemy of conceptual innovation. So my alternative strategy was to create a small, multi-disciplinary, multi-generational atelier with little hierarchy and few fixed roles. Anyone was free to comment on or contribute to any aspect of the project. Experts on particular topics took on the responsibility, as necessary, of bringing everyone up to speed on them. When some issue came up that was outside the current expertise of the group, one member assumed responsibility for quickly researching it and then educating all the others. The group had its own workspace and met frequently. It functioned as a face-to-face, peer-to-peer, just-in-time learning network with very intense internal interconnections.

The material culture of the group's workspace was important. This produced an accumulation of sketches, models, and prototypes. These were constantly available as reminders of previous discussions and decisions, as inspiration and reference, for tinkering and experimentation, and for demonstration and explanation.

This face-to-face network, in its information-rich spatial setting, was augmented by a digital network. Each member carried a wireless laptop and constantly used it. Through email, etc., this added a remote, asynchronous component to the group's interactions, and allowed it to continue functioning cohesively when members were scattered. In addition, there was a Wiki-like online repository of notes, sketches, reference material, CAD files, PowerPoint presentations and so on. Just about everything that the group did ended up in this continually evolving communal memory. (At later stages in design and construction projects, BIM (Building Information Modeling) systems often play similar roles.) This was the digital representation of the group's evolving and growing collective memory, and it was all available to anyone in the group, anywhere, anytime.

The group was, of course, embedded in larger spatial and online contexts, and its boundaries were permeable to those contexts. Spatially, the contexts were the MIT campus, the business and industrial environment of Cambridge, Massachusetts, and that of the Boston metropolitan area. These contexts contained many individuals, research groups, startup companies, consultants, and large industrial organisations with relevant expertise. Within this, there were networks of personal and professional connections, and formal and informal meeting places. A great deal of information and ideas flowed back and forth across the boundary between the group and these larger spatial environments—both enriching the group's learning and problem-solving and contributing to the functioning of the campus, Cambridge, and the Boston area as creative clusters.

The online context was that of the entire Web, and interactions with this occurred in multiple ways. Whenever some issue was raised during a group discussion, for example, someone would immediately Google it and inject the results back into the discussion in real time. Whenever some unusual part or material was needed for a prototype, someone would immediately try to find it on eBay or the Web page of some supplier—in effect, going to a global parts bin.

There were, of course, distant collaborators—in this case, mostly, in Detroit, Los Angeles, and Taiwan. These were kept in touch asynchronously through email and through pointers to relevant files on the group's server. Where necessary, there was synchronous communication through videoconferencing, Skype, and telephone. Often, these various synchronous and asynchronous modes were combined to support conversations among participants scattered at multiple points around the world.

Physical models and prototypes were crucial to the creative process. In the early stages, these were mostly quick, rough, and non-functional—made from inexpensive materials like cardboard and foam, and recorded with digital cameras. As concepts developed, three-dimensional Computer Aided Design (CAD) models became the core representations. These could be mounted on the server for joint access, downloaded at distant locations where necessary, and used in conjunction with laser cutters and deposition printers to produce physical models. With still further development,

	Synchronous	Asynchronous
Local	Face-to-face meetings and discussions	Reference to accumulated sketches, models, and prototypes in the physical workspace
Remote	Skype, telephone, videoconferencing	Web, email, voicemail

semi-functional prototypes in wood and plastic were produced from the CAD models by CAD/Computer Aided Manufacturing (CAM) devices. Finally, fully functional prototypes in metal were produced from the CAD models by Computer Numerical Control (CNC) machinery. Sometimes, parts were produced at scattered locations where the necessary capabilities existed, and then sent by express package to assembly points. These artefacts were not trashed or allowed to become scattered, but were preserved in the workplace.

In sum, the group learned and worked creatively by means of multiple modes of communication, as illustrated by the following table.

Notice that these various modes provide different learning and creative work opportunities, kinds and intensities of emotional expressiveness, direct costs, opportunity costs, and opportunities for multi-tasking. There is some overlap of functionality, so it is sometimes possible to substitute one for another, as for example when a videoconference substitutes for making a trip to meet face-to-face. But there are many differences, so their roles are mostly complementary rather than mutually substitutable. For example, quick, inexpensive, asynchronous email is often used to arrange expensive, high opportunity cost, face-to-face meetings.

These modes operating jointly and simultaneously constitute today's emerging environments for supporting creative work and learning. These environments have workshops, studios, and meeting places for face-to-face. They provide for accumulating collections of models, prototypes, and other physical work objects. They enable remote asynchronous interaction anywhere, anytime, from mobile wireless devices—mostly not, as in previous eras, from specialised, scheduled places like videoconferencing suites. And they are held together 24/7, independently of location, by the ubiquitous "glue" of Web access and email.

Meeting places, collections of physical artefacts, and sites of specialised equipment and resources give specific spatial structure to these environments. But the various sites are not closed, like old-fashioned classrooms and ateliers; instead they are electronically permeable, and physically interconnected by the mobility of group members and the rapid transfer of physical products among sites. They are organised in concentric zones, with the innermost zone (the group workspace) depending heavily upon face-to-face interaction and direct contact with materials and equipment, and successively more distant layers—local, regional, and global—relying more and more upon remote and asynchronous electronic connection.

These new environments encourage multimodal multitasking, such as surfing the Web or emailing from wireless laptops in the classroom—practises that may conflict with norms and attitudes inherited from previous eras. They favour peer-to-peer learning and individual initiative over centralised dissemination of knowledge.

And, because of their permeability, they are not friendly to authoritarian teaching or group leadership—the teacher or master who, by virtue of greater knowledge than anyone else right there—rules within a classroom or closed, local domain. This demands new teaching and leadership styles.

Traditional business and academic strategies for concealing, protecting, and charging for intellectual property tend to conflict with the permeability of these environments, and to inhibit their effectiveness. But things are changing. The software field has successfully pioneered open source strategies. Despite the efforts of the recording industry to suppress them, musicians have developed strategies of creative audio filesharing. The Web encourages all manner of mashups. And MIT has developed Open Courseware on a large scale.

These sorts of learning and creative environments have emerged first in professional and research settings where the demands for quick learning and innovative production are great, the participants are selected and sophisticated, and the necessary resources are readily available. But I see no fundamental reason why they should not spread from the tertiary to the secondary and primary levels. The necessary technology is getting cheaper and much more widely available, and social and cultural norms are changing as children grow up with electronic environments. It will be very interesting when they get right down to the kindergartens.

Suggested Reading

General

"Barker Review of Land Use Planning", Department of Communities and Local Government, 2006.

Florida, Richard, *The Rise of the Creative Class*, London: Basic Books, 2002.

Foxell Simon, ed., *The professionals' choice: The future of the built environment professions*, London: Building Futures, 2003.

Kunstler, James Howard, *The Long Emergency*, Atlantic Monthly Press, 2005.

Leadbeater, Charles, *Personalisation through participation: A new script for public services*, London: Demos, 2004.

Schumacher, EF, *Small is Beautiful*, Vancouver: Hartley & Marks,1999.

Economic Survey of the United Kingdom, OECD, 2007.

World Population Prospects: The 2006 Revision, Population Division of the Department of Economic and Social Affairs of the United Nations Secretariat, United Nations, 2007.

Planet Earth and Climate Change

Flannery, Tim, *The Weather Makers: The History and Future Impact of Climate Change*, Melbourne: Text Publishing, 2005.

Gore, Al, *Earth in the Balance: Ecology and the Human Spirit*, Boston: Houghton Mifflin, 1992.

Gore, Al, *The Assault on Reason*, Harmondsworth: Penguin, 2007.

Hartmann, Thom, *Last Hours of Ancient Sunlight*, New York: Three Rivers Press, 1997 (rev. 2004).

Hawken, Lovins & Lovins, *Natural Capitalism*, London: Little Brown, 1999.

Hillman, Mayer, *How We Can Save the Planet*, Harmondsworth: Penguin, 2004.

Homer-Dixon, Thomas, *The Upside of Down: Catastrophe, Creativity and the Renewal of Civilisation*, New York: Alfred A Knopf, 2006.

Kolbert, Elizabeth, *Field Notes from a Catastrophe: A Frontline Report on Climate Change*, London: Bloomsbury, 2006.

Lovelock, James, *Gaia: A New Look at Life on Earth*, Oxford: Oxford University Press, 1979.

Lovelock, James, *The Revenge of Gaia*, London: Allen Lane, 2006.

Lynas, Mark, *High Tide: The Truth About Our Climate Crisis*, London: Picador, 2004.

Lynas, Mark, *Six Degrees: Our Future on a Hotter Planet*, London: Fourth Estate, 2007.

Marshall, George, *Carbon Detox*, London: Gaia Thinking, 2007.

McDonough, W, and Braungert M, *Cradle to Cradle, Remaking the Way We Make Things*, New York: North Point Press, 2002.

Monbiot, George, *Heat: How We Can Stop the Planet Burning*, London: Allen Lane, 2006.

Walker, G, and King D, *The Hot Topic: How to Tackle Global Warming and Still Keep the Lights On*, London: Bloomsbury, 2008.

Action Today to Protect Tomorrow—The Mayor's Climate Change Action Plan, London: GLA, 2007.

Climate Change The UK Programme, London: DEFRA, 2006.

Summary for Policymakers of the Synthesis Report of the IPCC Fourth Assessment Report, United Nations, 2007.

Cities

Girardet, Herbert, *Cities People Planet: Liveable Cities for a Sustainable World*, Chichester: Wiley-Academy, 2004.

Jacobs, Jane, *The Death and Life of Great American Cities*, New York: Random House, 1961.

Jacobs, Jane, *The Economy of Cities*, New York: Random House, 1969.

Mumford, Lewis, *The Culture of Cities*, New York: Secker & Warburg, 1938.

Sudjic, Deyan, "Cities on the edge of chaos", *The Observer*, March 2008.

Urban Task Force, *Towards an Urban Renaissance*, London: E&FN Spon, 1999.

Work

Abramson, Daniel M,
*Building the Bank of
England*, New Haven, CT:
Yale University Press, 2005.

Alexander, Christopher, *The
Timeless Way of Building*,
Oxford: Oxford University
Press, 1979.

Anderson, Ray, *Mid-Course
Correction: The Interface
Model*, Chelsea Green,
2007.

Brand, Stewart, *How Buildings
Learn*, New York: Viking Press,
1994.

Brinkley, Ian, *Defining the
Knowledge Economy,
Knowledge Economy
Programme Report*, London:
The Work Foundation, 2006.

Castells, Manuel,
*The Information Age:
Economy, Society, Culture*,
Oxford: Blackwell, 1996.

Davenport, *Tom, Thinking
for a Living*, Boston: Harvard
Business School Press, 2005.

Dodgson, Gann, and Salter,
Think, Play, Do, Oxford, 2005.

Dodgson, Gann and
Salter, *The management of
technological innovation
strategy and practice*, Oxford:
Oxford University Press, 2008.

Duffy, Francis, *The Changing
Workplace*, London: Phaidon,
1992.

Duffy, Francis, *The New Office*,
London: Conran Octopus, 1997.

Duffy, Francis,
Architectural Knowledge,
London: E&FN Spon, 1998.

Duffy, Cave, Worthington, *Planning
Office Space*, London: The
Architectural Press, 1976.

Galloway, L, *Office Management:
Its Principles and Practice*, Oxford:
The Ronald Press, 1918.

Gann, David, *Building Innovation*,
London: Thomas Telford, 2000.

Giedion, Siegfried, *Mechanization
Takes Command*, Oxford: Oxford
University Press, 1948.

Gilbreth, FB, *Motion Study*, New
York: Van Nostrand, 1911.

Gottfried, David, *Greed to Green*,
Berkeley, CA: Worldbuild Publishing,
2004.

Groak, Steven, *Is Construction
an Industry?*, Construction
Management and Economics,
1994.

Handy, Charles, *Understanding
Organizations*, Harmondsworth:
Penguin, 1967.

Hawken, Paul, *The Ecology
of Commerce*, New York:
HarperCollins, 1993.

Mitchell, William J, *City of Bits*, Cambridge, MA: MIT Press, 1995.

Quinan, Jack, *Frank Lloyd Wright's Larkin Building*, Cambridge, MA: MIT Press, 1987.

Sassen, Saskia, *A Sociology of Globalization*, New York: Norton, 2006.

Sennett, Richard, *The Culture of the New Capitalism*, New Haven, CT: Yale University Press, 2006.

Taylor, Frederick, *The Principles of Scientific Management*, New York: Harper & Brothers, 1911.

Trease, Geoffrey, *Samuel Pepys and His World*, London: Thames and Hudson, 1972.

Education

Aston and Bekhradnia, *Demand for Graduates: A review of the economic evidence*, Higher Education Policy Institute, 2003.

Friere, Paolo, *Education: the practice of freedom*, London: Writers and Readers Cooperative, 1974.

Gardner, Howard, *Multiple Intelligences*, New York: Basic Books, 1993.

Goodman, Paul, *Growing up absurd*, New York: First Sphere Books, 1970.

Illich, Ivan, *Deschooling Society*, London: Calder and Boyars.1971.

Kimber, Mike, Does Size Matter? *Distributed leadership in small secondary schools*, National College for School Leadership, 2003.

Nair and Fielding, *The Language of School Design*, DesignShare, 2005.

Neil, AS, Summerhill, Harmondsworth: Penguin Books,1968. *The Children's Plan—Building Brighter Futures*, DCSF, December 2007.

Every Child Matters: Change for Children, DfES/HM Government, 2004.

Higher Standards, Better Schools For All, DfES.

2020 Vision Report of the Teaching and Learning in 2020, Review Group, 2006.

www.smallschools.org.uk

www.thecademy.net/ inclusiontrust.org/ Welcome.html

www.eco-schools.org.uk

www.standards.dfes.gov.uk/
personalisedlearning/about/

Transport and Neighbourhoods

Banister, David, *Unsustainable Transport: City Transport in the New Century*, London: E&FN Spon, 2005.

Bertolini L, and T, Spit, *Cities on Rails. The Redevelopment of Railway Station Areas*, London: Spon/Routledge, 1998.

Calthorpe P, and Fulton, W, *The Regional City: Planning for the End of Sprawl*, Washington, DC: Island Press, 2003.

Dittmar H, and Ohland, G, *The New Transit Town: Best Practices in Transit-Oriented Development*, Washington, DC: Island Press, 2004.

Hickman, R and Banister, D, *Looking over the horizon, Transport and reduced CO_2 emissions in the UK by 2030*, Transport Policy, 2007.

Holtzclaw, Clear, Dittmar, Goldstein and Haas, *Location Efficiency: Neighborhood and Socioeconomic Characteristics Determine Auto Ownership and Use*, Transportation Planning and Technology (Vol. 25) 2002.

Commission for Integrated Transport, Planning for

High Speed Rail Needed Now, 2004, viewed at http://www.cfit.gov.uk/pn/040209/index.htm

Regional Transport Statistics, National Statistics and Department for Transport, 2006 Edition.

Energy, Transport and Environment Indicators, Eurostat, 2005 Edition.

Toward a Sustainable Transport system, Department for Transport, 2007.

Eddington Transport Study, HM Treasury & Department for Transport, 2007.

UK Foresight programme, *Tackling Obesities: Future Choices*, The Government Office for Science and Technology, 2007.

Community

Dench G, Gavron K, and Young M, *The New East End: Kinship, Race and Conflict*, London: Profile, 2006.

Jacobs, Jane, *The Death and Life of American Cities*, New York: Modern Library, 1961.

Putnam, Robert, *Bowling Alone: The Collapse and Revival of American Community*, New York: Simon & Schuster, 2000.

Young M, and Willmott, P, *Family and Kinship in East London*, Harmondsworth: Penguin, 1957.

Report Card 7, *Child poverty in perspective: An overview of child well-being in rich countries*, UNICEF Innocenti Research Centre, 2007.

Key Facts for Diverse Communities: Ethnicity and Faith, Greater London Authority, Data Management and Analysis Group, 2007.

www.footprintnetwork.org

www.yourhistoryhere

www.fixmystreet.com

Globalisation

Abbott, C, Rogers, P, Sloboda, J, *Global Responses to Global Threats: Sustainable Security for the 21st Century*, Oxford: The Oxford Research Group, 2006.

Balls E, Healey J and Leslie C, *Evolution and Devolution in England*, New Local Government Network, 2006.

Gladwell, Malcolm, *The Tipping Point: How Little Things Can Make a Big Difference*, London: Little Brown, 2000.

Goldsmith, Edward, "How to Feed People under a Regime of Climate Change", *Ecologist Magazine*, 2004.

Gore, Al, *The Assault on Reason*, London: Bloomsbury, 2007.

Gray, John, *Black Mass: Apocalyptic Religion and the Death of Utopia*, London: Allen Lane, 2007.

Guillebaud, John, Youthquake: *Population, Fertility and Environment in the 21st Century*, Optimum Population Trust, 2007.

Hines, Colin, *Localisation: A Global Manifesto*, London: Earthscan, 2000.

Kagan, Robert, *Of Paradise and Power: America and Europe in the New World Order*, New York: Alfred Knopf, 2003.

Martin, James, *The Meaning of the 21st Century*, London: Transworld, 2007.

Meadows, Meadows, Randers and Behrens, *Limits to Growth*, Club of Rome, 1972.

Nordhaus, T, and M, Shellenberger, *Break Through: From the Death of Environmentalism to the Politics of Possibility*, Boston: Houghton Mifflin, 2007.

Porritt, Jonathon, *Capitalism: As if the World Matters*, London: Earthscan, 2005.

Roszak, Theodore, *World Beware! American Triumphalism in an Age of Terror*, Toronto: Between the Lines, 2006.

Sachs, W, and T, Santarius *Fair Future: Resource Conflicts, Security and Global Justice*, London: Zed Books, 2005.

Kirkpatrick Sale, *Dwellers in the Land*, New Society Publishers, 1991.

Shrybman, Steven, *A Citizen's Guide to the World Trade Organisation*, Ottawa, Canadian Center for Policy Alternatives, 1999.

Soros, George, *The Age of Fallability: The Consequences of the War on Terror*, Beverly Hills, CA: Phoenix Books, 2006.

Stern, Nicholas, *The Economics of Climate Change: The Stern Review*, Cambridge: Cambridge University Press, 2007.

Stiglitz, Joseph, *Globalization and its Discontents*, New York: Norton, 2002.

Stiglitz, Joseph, *Making Globalization Work*, New York: Norton, 2006.

Wolf, Martin, *Why Globalization Works*, New Haven, CT: Yale University Press, 2005.

Johannesburg Manifesto, Fairness in a Fragile World, Berlin: Heinrich Böll Foundation, 2002.

US Defence Dept, *An Abrupt Climate Change Scenario and It's Implications for US Natural Security*, 2003.

WWF, Living Planet Report, WWF International, 2006.

Further websites

The Edge
www.at-the-edge.org.uk

CABE
www.cabe.org.uk

China Dialogue
www.chinadialogue.net

Global Commons Institute (Contraction and Convergence)
www.gci.org.uk

Authors

Robin Nicholson
Robin Nicholson CBE is a senior director of Edward
Cullinan Architects and a Commissioner of CABE. He is
a past chair of the Construction Industry Council and is a
founder member of the Edge.

Simon Foxell
Simon Foxell is the founding principal of The Architects
Practice and a member of the Edge. He is a past chair
of Policy and Strategy at the RIBA and currently acts as
Design Advisor to Transforming Education, Birmingham
City Council. He is the author of the RIBA best practice
guide to Starting a practice, 2006, and *Mapping London:
making sense of the city*, 2007.

William J Mitchell
William J Mitchell is director of the MIT Design Laboratory
and directs the Media Lab's Smart Cities research group.
He was formerly dean of the School of Architecture and
Planning and head of the Program in Media Arts and
Sciences, both at MIT. He is the author of many books
including *City of Bits: Space, Place, and the Infobahn*, 1995.

The Edge

The Edge is a ginger group and think tank, sponsored by the building industry professions, that seeks to stimulate public interest in policy questions that affect the built environment, and to inform and influence public opinion. It was established in 1996 with support from the Arup Foundation. The Edge is supported by The Carbon Trust.

The Edge organises a regular series of debates and other events intended to advance policy thinking in the built environment sector and among the professional bodies within it. For further details, see www.at-the-edge.org.uk

Edge Futures

Edge Futures is a project initiated by The Edge and Black Dog
Publishing. It has only been possible with the active participation of
The Edge Committee as well as supporting firms and institutions.
Special thanks are due to Adam Poole, Duncan McCorquodale,
Frank Duffy, Robin Nicholson, Bill Gething, Chris Twinn, Andy Ford,
Mike Murray and Jane Powell as well as to all the individual authors.

The project has been generously sponsored by The Carbon Trust,
The Commission for Architecture and the Built Environment
(CABE), Ramboll Whitbybird, The Arup Foundation, ProLogis and
Construction Skills. Thanks are due to all those bodies and to the
support of Karen Germain, Elanor Warwick, Mark Whitby, Ken
Hall and Guy Hazlehurst within them. The Edge is also grateful to
Sebastian Macmillan of IDBE in Cambridge for the day we spent
developing scenarios there and to Philip Guildford for facilitating
the session.

Simon Foxell

Much is already known about the state of the world
15 to 20 years from now. Almost all the buildings and
infrastructure are already in place or in development—
we replace our buildings etc., at a very slow pace. The
great majority of the population who'll be living and
working then, especially in the UK, have already been
born and will have been educated in a school system
that is familiar and predictable. The global population,
however, will have increased from 6.7 billion in July 2007
to approximately 8 billion by 2025.

The climate will have changed, mainly as a result of the
emissions of greenhouse gases of the past 50 and more
years, but not by much. The temperature is predicted to
be, on average, half a degree warmer, as well as varying
over a greater range than at present. But, more significantly
it will be understood to be changing, resulting in a strong
feeling of uncertainty and insecurity. Rainfall will have
reduced but will also become more extreme, i.e. tending to
drought or flood. Resources, whether energy, water or food
imports, will be in shorter supply; partly as a result of
climate change but also due to regulations aimed at
preventing the effects of global warming becoming worse.
Transport will be constrained as a result but other
technologies will have greatly improved the ability to
economically communicate.

These changes form the context for this first series of
five Edge Futures books, but it is not their subject: that
is the impact of such changes and other developments
on our daily lives, the economy, social and education
services and the way the world trades and operates.
Decision makers are already being challenged to act
and formulate policy, in the face of the change already
apparent in the years ahead. This set of books highlights
how critical and important planning for the future is
going to be. Society will expect and require policy

makers to have thought ahead and prepared for the best as well as the worst. Edge Futures offers a series of critical views of events, in the next two decades, that need to be planned for today.

The five books intentionally look at the future from very different viewpoints and perspectives. Each author, or pair of authors, has been asked to address a different sector of society, but there is inevitably a great deal of crossover between them. They do not always agree; but consistency is not the intention; that is to capture a breadth of vision as where we may be in 20 years time.

Jonathon Porritt in *Globalism and Regionalism* examines some of the greatest challenges before the planet, including climate change and demographic growth, and lays down the gauntlet to the authors of the other books. Porritt's diagnosis of the need to establish a new balance between the global and the regional over the years ahead and to achieve a 'Civic Globalisation' has an echo in Geoff Mulgan's call in *Living and Community* for strengthening communities through rethinking local governance and rebuilding a sense of place. Both are—perhaps professionally—optimistic that the climate change is a challenge that we, as a society, can deal with, while not underestimating the change that our society is going to have to undergo to achieve it.

Hank Dittmar, writing in *Transport and Networks* is less than certain, that currently, policies are adequately joined-up to deal with the issues that the recent flurry of major reports from the UK Government has highlighted: "Planning" from Barker, "Climate Change" from Stern and "Transport" from Eddington. He notes Barker's comment that "planning plays a role in the mitigation of and adaptation to climate change, the biggest issue faced across all climate areas" but that she then goes on to dismiss the issue. In its approach to all these reviews, the government has shown that it is more concerned with economic growth and indeed it has already concluded that the transport network needs no further fundamental reform. Dittmar believes otherwise, he calls for immediate solutions to support the development of the accessible, sustainable city.

Simon Foxell in *Education and Creativity* sees an even bumpier ride ahead, with progress only being made as a result of the lurch from crisis to crisis. Such discontinuities, will allow the UK to address many longstanding problems, from the personalisation of education to addressing the increasingly cut-throat international competition in creativity, innovation and skills—but not without a great deal of pain and chaos. Bill Mitchell, in the same volume, outlines a way of reconfiguring educational practice to develop just those skills that successful creativity-based economies are going to require.

In *Working*, Frank Duffy sees the end of road for the classic 'American Taylorist' office and the unsuitability of its counterpart, the European social democratic office. In their place, he proposes a new typology—the networked office—that will make better use of the precious resource that is our existing stock of buildings and allow greater integration into the life of the city. And, it is the city that all the authors come back to as a central and unifying theme—the dominant form of the millennium, the place where the majority of mankind now lives. Perhaps this is because, as Deyan Sudjic, Director of the Design Museum, has written recently; "The future of the city has suddenly become the only subject in town."

It is about the largest social unit that most of us can imagine with any ease and is a constant challenge economically, socially and environmentally. If we can work out what a sustainable city might be like and how to deliver it, then maybe we can sleep easier in our beds, less afraid that the end of civilisation, as we recognise it, may be within our childrens', or our childrens' childrens', lifetime. All the component parts of the Edge Futures studies come together in the city; where the community meets the office buildings, the schools and transport system. The city is the hub of the regional response to world events and needs to become a responsive participant in formulating a way out of policy log-jam.

As this first series of Edge Futures shows, the task is urgent and deeply complex but also not impossible. It is only, assuming that we need to make the transition to a low carbon economy within ten to twenty years, in Geoff Mulgan's words: "extraordinarily challenging by any historic precedent."

10a Acton Street
London WC1X 9NG
T. +44 (0)20 7613 1922
F. +44 (0)20 7613 1944
E. info@blackdogonline.com
W. www.blackdogonline.com

Designed by Draught Associates

All opinions expressed within this publication are those of the authors and
not necessarily of the publisher.

British Library Cataloguing-in-Publication Data.
A CIP record for this book is available from the British Library.
ISBN: 978 1 906155 100

Black Dog Publishing, London, UK is an environmentally responsible
company. Edge Futures are printed on Cyclus Offset, a paper produced
from 100% post consumer waste.

architecture art design
fashion history photography
theory and things

www.blackdogonline.com